BARRY GIBB

: The Man Behind The Music Journey through Decades of Musical Brilliance.

Fred W Smith

Barry Gibb

TABLE OF CONTENT

Barry Gibb

INTRODUCTION

"Barry Gibb: The Man Behind the Music" takes you inside the remarkable life of a musical icon whose influence spans generations in the engrossing pages that follow. The fascinating story of Barry Gibb's journey is revealed in this book, which starts in the modest Australian town of Redcliffe and ends at the height of international fame.

Explore the intricacies of his early life, when tenacity and passion created the basis for the recognizable sound that would reverberate for decades. Gibb's narrative, as the engine behind the venerable Bee Gees and a prolific solo artist, is a symphony of inventiveness, tenacity, and uncompromising devotion to the craft.

Explore the man behind the tunes beyond the spotlight and learn about his struggles, historical collaborations that influenced particular times, and lasting influence on the music industry. The documentary "The Man Behind the Music" presents a close-up view of Barry Gibb, encapsulating the spirit of a master whose harmonies endure forever.

As we explore the facets of Barry Gibb's life and honor the continuing legacy of a genuine musical

Barry Gibb

genius, come along on this journey through the highs and lows, the songs and memories.

CHAPTER 1: WHO IS BARRY GIBB?

Born on September 1, 1946, Barry Gibb is a British-Australian musician, singer, and songwriter. He is most recognized for being one of the original members, along with his brothers Robin and Maurice Gibb, of the legendary pop and disco trio the Bee Gees. With classics like "Stayin' Alive," "How Deep Is Your Love," and "Night Fever," the Bee Gees enjoyed enormous success and made a huge contribution to the late 1970s disco period.

In addition to his Bee Gees work, Barry Gibb has worked with a variety of musicians in a variety of genres and had a prosperous solo career. He has had a long-lasting impact on the music business and is well-known for his outstanding songwriting, unique voice, and contributions to the development of popular music. In the music industry, Barry Gibb is still regarded as a legend with a lasting impact.

1.1 Early life

Hugh and Barbara Gibb welcomed Barry Alan Crompton Gibb into the world on September 1, 1946, in Douglas, Isle of Man. In 1958, in search of a better life, his family relocated to Redcliffe, Australia. Barry was the firstborn among five children; his younger siblings, Andy and Lesley, were born after him and his brothers, Robin and Maurice.

The Gibb siblings showcased their musical abilities from a young age, and the Gibb family was always filled with music. The Gibb brothers created The Rattlesnakes, a rock and roll/skiffle group, during their teenage years. The family relocated to Manchester, England in 1960 to pursue a music career after realizing their potential.

The brothers continued to hone their skills in Manchester, where they gave minor performances at neighborhood places and gained a fan base. After returning to Redcliffe in 1967, the Bee Gees made their official debut on the global music scene. Their career took off after the publication of "New York Mining Disaster 1941," which served as their breakthrough.

A key component of the Bee Gees' popularity was Barry Gibb's distinctive falsetto voice, which he used as a lead vocalist and prolific songwriter. Early on in the group's history, they experimented with a variety of musical genres, such as pop, folk, and rock.

Barry Gibb

The Gibb brothers' strong relationship catalyzed their inventiveness. Barry's guidance combined with the distinctive qualities of Robin and Maurice created the dynamic that would go on to become the Bee Gees one of the most popular and enduring musical groups in history.

In addition to providing the groundwork for his musical career, Barry Gibb's early upbringing gave him the tenacity and willpower that defined his professional life. The Bee Gees' rise from an Australian local band to an international phenomenon is a credit to Barry Gibb's skill, perseverance, and the lasting influence of his early years.

1.2 Bee Gees Formation

The Gibb family's musical ambitions are where the Bee Gees got their start. Barry Gibb began his musical career in the late 1950s, together with his younger brothers Robin and Maurice. In 1958, the Isle of Man-born family relocated to Redcliffe, Australia, in search of improved living conditions.

During their formative years, the Gibb brothers demonstrated their musical abilities by participating in regional talent competitions and events. The trio formed The Rattlesnakes, a rock and roll/skiffle ensemble, out of their shared love of music. Barry, Robin, and Maurice showed off their amazing songwriting and harmonies even as young children.

Seeing that their music career had promise, the Gibb family relocated to Manchester, England in 1960. The brothers kept improving their craft, doing small-scale performances and winning praise from their community. During this time, they started going by the nickname "Bee Gees," which is an acronym for "Brothers Gibb."

Renowned entrepreneur Robert Stigwood noticed the Bee Gees while they were in England and offered them a management deal. In 1967, the family returned to Redcliffe, and the Bee Gees achieved worldwide recognition with the release of "New York Mining Disaster 1941." Their breakthrough track, which included their trademark close harmonies, signaled the start of their popularity.

The early Bee Gees sound was influenced by many musical styles, such as folk, pop, and rock. They kept developing as the 1960s went on, adding psychedelic aspects to their songs. Barry Gibb's direction and the individual talents of Robin and Maurice combined to produce a sound that would come to be associated with the Bee Gees.

Barry Gibb

The Bee Gees experimented with various musical genres in the late 1960s and early 1970s, setting the stage for their eventual triumph in the disco period. Their sound was characterized by Barry Gibb's falsetto vocals. The album "Saturday Night Fever," which included well-known hits like "Stayin' Alive" and "How Deep Is Your Love," was released in 1977, marking a turning point.

The Bee Gees' long-lasting popularity was largely due to the distinctive talents of his brothers and Barry Gibb's role as lead vocalist and key songwriter. The Bee Gees' founding symbolizes a journey from Redcliffe's little stages to global prominence, having a lasting impression on the popular music scene.

CHAPTER 2: MUSICAL CAREER

Barry Gibb's musical career has been an amazing journey, characterized by his prolific songwriting, unique voice, and long-lasting popularity as a solo artist as well as a member of the Bee Gees. This is a thorough analysis of his musical career:

1. The Bee Gees in Their Early Years:

In the late 1950s, Barry Gibb, and his brothers Robin and Maurice, created the Bee Gees. In an attempt to pursue a music career, they relocated from Australia to England during their formative years. The brothers' distinct style and harmonies won them praise, which led to a management deal with Robert Stigwood.

2. Sound's Evolution:

Throughout the 1960s, the Bee Gees' sound changed from rock and pop to incorporate elements of folk and psychedelic music. Barry's ability to write songs came through, and the group's music gained a special depth from his unusual falsetto voice.

3. Important Turning Points and Global Pioneers:

Barry Gibb

The Bee Gees experienced a sea change when "New York Mining Disaster 1941" was released in 1967 and helped to establish them on a global scale. Hits like "To Love Somebody" and "Massachusetts" kept coming from them.

4. Dominance of Disco Era:

The Bee Gees shot to international fame in 1977 thanks to their significant contribution to the "Saturday Night Fever" soundtrack. Barry Gibb's falsetto vocals on singles like "How Deep Is Your Love" and "Stayin' Alive" made the disco period famous.

5. Independent Career:

Late in the 1970s and early in the 1980s, Barry Gibb took the step into becoming a solo artist. "Flowing Rivers" and "Barry Gibb Now Voyager," two of his solo albums, demonstrated his versatility outside of the disco sound of the Bee Gees.

6. Songwriting and Collaborations:

Barry Gibb was not just a talented songwriter for the Bee Gees; he also wrote songs for other singers in different genres. His versatility was demonstrated by his collaborations, which included pop with Barbra Streisand and country music with Kenny Rogers.

7. The Comeback of Bee Gees and Their Later Years:

In the late 1980s, the Bee Gees saw a comeback thanks to singles like "One" and "You Win Again." Barry Gibb carried on his brother's legacy by performing solo occasionally, even after Maurice and Robin passed away in 2003 and 2012, respectively.

8. Accolades & Honours:

Throughout their career, Barry Gibb and the Bee Gees won a plethora of accolades, including Grammys, Brit Awards, and inductions into the Rock and Roll Hall of Fame. A Lifetime Achievement Award was given in recognition of their contribution to music.

9. Historical Background:

Barry Gibb's influence on succeeding musical generations goes well beyond the disco era. His contributions to the Bee Gees' sound and his solo activities further cemented his place in music history.

Barry Gibb

Barry Gibb's musical career is a monument to inventiveness, flexibility, and fortitude; he has left a lasting impression on popular music history.

2.1 Bee Gees Hits

As a member of the Bee Gees, Barry Gibb was instrumental in producing some of the most well-known songs in popular music history. Here's a thorough examination of a few of the important Bee Gees songs:

1. The 1967 song "To Love Somebody":

Barry Gibb's expressive vocals were highlighted in this soulful ballad, which solidified the Bee Gees' status as more than just a pop group.

2. "Massachusetts" (1967): One of the Bee Gees' first defining songs, "Massachusetts" caught the mournful beauty of their harmonies and went on to become a chart-topping success.

3. The 1968 song "I've Gotta Get a Message to You":

This poignant ballad showcased Barry's and the Bee Gees' storytelling skills as well as their ability to express intricate storylines via song.

4. 1968's "Words":

"Words" further demonstrated Barry Gibb's songwriting abilities and the group's developing sound with its lyrical lyrics and melodic beauty.

5. "I Started a Joke" (1968): Barry's eerie vocals and the song's reflective lyrics revealed a new side to the Bee Gees' repertoire.

6. In 1970, "Lonely Days":

This early 1970s success showcased the Bee Gees' versatility as they combined their trademark harmonies with pop and rock elements.

7. "How Can You Mend a Broken Heart" (1971): Barry's capacity to emote deeply is demonstrated in this heartbreaking ballad, which went on to become one of the Bee Gees' first number-one successes in the United States.

8. The 1975 song "Jive Talkin'":

"Jive Talkin'" signaled a style change for the Bee Gees as they moved into the disco period, bringing in funk influences and setting the stage for their eventual triumph.

9. 1975's "Nights on Broadway":

Barry Gibb

In this disco-infused song, Barry's vocals stole the show and cemented the Bee Gees' reputation as genre pioneers.

10. The 1977 song "Stayin' Alive":

With Barry's distinctive falsetto, "Stayin' Alive" from the "Saturday Night Fever" soundtrack is arguably the most famous Bee Gees song and came to represent the disco era.

11. The 1977 song "How Deep Is Your Love":

A timeless smash from the "Saturday Night Fever" soundtrack that highlights both the Bee Gees' timeless songwriting and Barry's soulful voice.

12. 1977's "Night Fever":

"Night Fever" became a disco classic thanks to its catchy beat and Barry's falsetto vocals, which helped the Bee Gees dominate the charts at the time.

13. The 1978 song "Too Much Heaven":

This ballad, with Barry's vocals soaring above lush harmonies, demonstrated the Bee Gees' ability to write songs that resonate deeply emotionally.

These songs not only shaped the Bee Gees' career but also cemented Barry Gibb's standing as a talented singer and songwriter, making a lasting impression on popular music.

2.2 Solo Projects

Outside of the Bee Gees, Barry Gibb has continued to write and sing a great deal of songs and has ventured into a variety of musical styles during his solo career. Here's a thorough examination of Barry Gibb's solo endeavors:

1. "The Kid's No Good" (1970): Barry Gibb's first solo album, "The Kid's No Good," explored a more rock-oriented sound, showing off a divergence from the Bee Gees' sound. However, there was little commercial success for the album.

2. Solo Recordings in the Later Seventies:

Barry Gibb recorded many solo albums, including "Flowing Rivers" (1977) and "Shadow Dancing" (1980), after the Bee Gees' disco era breakthrough. Hits from "Flowing Rivers" included "I Just Want to Be Your Everything," which peaked at the top of the US charts.

3. 1980's "Guilty":

Barry Gibb

The title track and other successes from the album "Guilty," which Barry Gibb and Barbra Streisand collaborated on, include "What Kind of Fool." The record was a huge hit and demonstrated Gibb's adaptability and genre-bending skills.

4. Songwriting and Collaborations:

Barry Gibb persisted in working with different musicians, lending his compositional abilities to endeavors not associated with the Bee Gees. Among the most notable partnerships was their work on Kenny Rogers' popular album "Eyes That See in the Dark," which included the timeless song "Islands in the Stream."

5. The 1984 film "Now Voyager":

Barry Gibb continued his experimentation with many musical genres with his solo album "Now Voyager". Even though it wasn't as commercially successful as his previous solo endeavors, it showed his continued dedication to solo endeavors.

6. Composing Music for Other Performers:

Barry Gibb was also a talented songwriter who wrote songs for other musicians, including Diana Ross's "Chain Reaction" and Dionne Warwick's "Heartbreaker".

Barry Gibb

7. (2016) "In the Now":

"In the Now," Barry Gibb's first solo album of brand-new songs in more than 30 years, was released in 2016. The record retained aspects of his traditional songwriting while showcasing a modern feel.

8. Live Exhibitions:

Barry Gibb has periodically gone solo, putting on live performances that feature a blend of his hits as a solo artist, iconic Bee Gees songs, and timeless group collaborations.

Through his solo endeavors, Barry Gibb has been able to experiment with a variety of musical styles, showcasing his versatility and unwavering creative energy. Even though the Bee Gees will always hold a special place in his heart, his solo endeavors reveal a breadth of brilliance that goes beyond the group's signature sound.

CHAPTER 3: SONGWRITING

Barry Gibb's lasting influence in the music business is largely due to his skill as a songwriter. His talent for creating unforgettable melodies and sad lyrics has made a lasting impression on popular music. This is an in-depth analysis of Barry Gibb's songwriting:

1. Formative Years and Working with Brothers:

Songwriting was always a natural skill of Barry Gibb's, even in the early Bee Gees days. Together with his brothers Maurice and Robin, the trio developed into a strong songwriting partnership. Hits like "To Love Somebody" and "Massachusetts" from their early catalog demonstrated Barry's ability to emote via songwriting.

2. Emotional resonance and lyrical depth:

Barry Gibb frequently explores themes of love, heartache, and reflection in his songwriting. Because of the literary quality of his lyrics, audiences may relate to the deep feelings expressed in songs like "How Can You Mend a Broken Heart" and "I Started a Joke."

Barry Gibb

3. Style's Evolution:

Barry's songwriting technique changed over the years in tandem with the Bee Gees' musical development. His versatility was evident in his songs from the 1960s folk-inspired hits to the late 1970s dance anthems, all while retaining the richness of the lyrics and melody that defined his sound.

4. A Successful Disco Era:

Writing the disco hits that defined a period for the Bee Gees was a major contribution from Barry Gibb. Not only did songs like "Stayin' Alive," "How Deep Is Your Love," and "Night Fever" dominate the charts, but they also showed how well Barry could write songs that encapsulated the era.

5. Working Together Outside of the Bee Gees:

Barry Gibb was a talented songwriter outside of the Bee Gees. He wrote successes such as "Islands in the Stream" for Kenny Rogers and Dolly Parton and "Heartbreaker" for Dionne Warwick while working with other musicians. These partnerships demonstrated his ability in a variety of genres.

6. Contemplating Individual Experiences:

Barry Gibb

Barry Gibb gets inspiration for a lot of his songs from his thoughts and experiences. His ageless style is a result of his ability to bring genuineness to his lyrics.

7. Acknowledgments and Honours:

Barry Gibb's accomplishments as a songwriter are well known. Barry and the other members of The Bee Gees were honored with multiple accolades for their musical accomplishments, including being inducted into the Songwriters Hall of Fame.

8. Generational Impact:

The songwriting of Barry Gibb has had a significant impact on performers in later generations. His influence will last a lifetime because of his ability to write timeless songs and words that touch on universal subjects.

9. One-Man Songwriting Initiatives:

Barry Gibb persisted in writing songs on his own, collaborating with Barbra Streisand on albums like "Guilty" and producing solo singles like "In the Now" in 2016.

Barry Gibb's lasting contribution to popular music is evidence of his exceptional creative talent, as evidenced by his songwriting legacy. Being able to combine storytelling, melody, and emotion seamlessly has made him one of the greatest songwriters in music history.

3.1 Achievements

Barry Gibb's accomplishments are multifaceted and include his outstanding work as a musician, songwriter, and Bee Gees member. This is a thorough examination of Barry Gibb's accomplishments:

1. The dominance of Bee Gees on the Chart:

Along with his brothers Robin and Maurice, Barry Gibb was a founding member of the Bee Gees and was instrumental in the group's hit-making success. With multiple songs in pop, rock, and disco, the Bee Gees gained recognition on a global scale.

2. Grammy Honours:

Throughout their careers, the Bee Gees and Barry Gibb won numerous Grammy Awards. They have won awards for Album of the Year, Record of the Year, and Best Pop Performance by a Duo or Group with Vocal, among other titles.

Barry Gibb

3. Soundtrack for "Saturday Night Fever":

With classics like "Stayin' Alive" and "How Deep Is Your Love," the Bee Gees' contribution to the "Saturday Night Fever" soundtrack is a historic accomplishment. Not only did the soundtrack turn into one of the all-time best-selling albums, but it also helped to define the disco era.

4. Induction into the Songwriters Hall of Fame:

In 1994, Barry Gibb and his siblings were admitted into the Songwriters Hall of Fame. This honor highlights the songwriting duo's significant influence on the music business.

5. Awards for Lifetime Achievement:

Many notable lifetime achievement awards were given to The Bee Gees, particularly Barry Gibb, in recognition of their long-lasting influence on the music industry. These include accolades such as the Outstanding Contribution to Music (Brit Award).

6. Induction into the Rock and Roll Hall of Fame:

In 1997, the Rock & Roll Hall of Fame admitted The Bee Gees, honoring their noteworthy contributions to the development of popular music.

7. Guinness World Records:

Barry Gibb and the Bee Gees were the group with the most consecutive Hot 100 number-one hits in the United States, earning a spot in the Guinness World Records.

8. A Lucrative Individual Career:

Barry Gibb's solo career, which includes hits like "Flowing Rivers," "Guilty," and "In the Now," demonstrates his longevity in the music industry even after the Bee Gees broke up. Critical praise and chart-topping singles are among his solo accomplishments.

9. Effect on Various Genres:

Due to his flexibility as a performer and songwriter, Barry Gibb was able to create a big impact in a lot of different genres, like pop, rock, disco, and country music.

10. Charitable Activities:

Barry Gibb has participated in charitable activities, supporting causes including healthcare and music education. His dedication to giving back highlights his influence outside of the music industry.

Barry Gibb

Barry Gibb's accomplishments highlight his impact on popular music culture in addition to the Bee Gees' commercial success. His timeless impact as a humanitarian, singer, and musician is still felt by listeners all over the world.

3.2 Awards

Barry Gibb has won multiple accolades for his outstanding contributions to the music business, both as a member of the Bee Gees and in his solo career. This is a thorough analysis of Barry Gibb's accolades:

1. Grammy Awards: Throughout their career, The Bee Gees, which included Barry Gibb, was honored with several Grammy Awards. These include Best Pop Performance by a Duo or Group with Vocal, Record of the Year, and Album of the Year awards.

2. Brit Awards: In recognition of their substantial influence on the British music landscape, The Bee Gees were given the Brit Award for Outstanding Contribution to Music.

3. The Bee Gees were recognized for their efforts with multiple American Music Awards, including Favourite Pop/Rock Album and Favourite Soul/R&B Album.

4. Songwriters Hall of Fame: In 1994, Barry Gibb and his brothers were admitted into the Songwriters Hall of Fame, a recognition of their contribution to the songwriting profession.

5. Rock and Roll Hall of Fame: In 1997, The Bee Gees, which included Barry Gibb, were inducted into the Hall, solidifying their reputation as significant personalities in the annals of popular music.

The Bee Gees were granted the Ivor Novello Award for International Hit of the Year in recognition of their song "Massachusetts."

7. Grammy Hall of Fame: The Grammy Hall of Fame has admitted many Bee Gees recordings, including "How Deep Is Your Love" and "Stayin' Alive," which is evidence of the group's enduring influence.

8. CBE (Commander of the Order of the British Empire): In recognition of his contributions to music and charitable work, Barry Gibb was named a Commander of the Order of the British Empire (CBE) in 2004.

9. Australian Recording Business Association (ARIA) Hall of Fame: The Bee Gees received

recognition for their exceptional achievements in the Australian music business when they were inducted into the ARIA Hall of Fame.

10. Hollywood Walk of Fame: In recognition of their contributions to the recording business, The Bee Gees were bestowed with a star on the Hollywood Walk of Fame in 1997.

The Bee Gees hold the Guinness World Record for the most consecutive Hot 100 number-one hits in the United States (**11. Guinness World Records:**).

12. BMI Awards: For their accomplishments in songwriting and performance, Barry Gibb and the Bee Gees were recognized with multiple BMI Awards.

Barry Gibb's remarkable collection of accolades is a testament to the Bee Gees' financial success as well as their significant impact on the world of music. His lasting efforts are still honored and acknowledged on many esteemed forums.

CHAPTER 4: PERSONAL LIFE

In his personal life, Barry Gibb has been characterized by his family, enduring connections, and a strong love of music. This is a thorough examination of Barry Gibb's private life:

1. Background in the Family:

Hugh and Barbara Gibb welcomed Barry Alan Crompton Gibb into the world on September 1, 1946, in Douglas, Isle of Man. Among his siblings were three brothers, Maurice, Andy, and Lesley; he was the oldest of the five.

2. Sibling Relationships:

The Gibb brothers were a close-knit musical group that went by the name of the Bee Gees. The success of the ensemble was greatly influenced by their close relationship, with Barry frequently assuming a leadership position.

3. Matrimony and Offspring:

Before Linda Grey passed away in 2012, Barry Gibb and Linda Grey had a close relationship. They were married in 1970. Together, they were parents to five children: Alexandra, Ashley, Travis, Michael, and Stephen. Barry's family has supported him throughout his career and has been a vital part of his life.

4. Misfortunes and Death:

The deaths of his younger brothers, Andy Gibb in 1988, Maurice Gibb in 2003, and Robin Gibb in 2012, caused Barry Gibb to suffer a great deal of personal loss. Barry was greatly impacted by these setbacks on a personal and professional level.

5. Durability and Legacy Preservation:

Barry Gibb showed resiliency by carrying on the Bee Gees' legacy via concerts, interviews, and sporadic solo endeavors in spite of the difficulties and heartaches. One touching part of his journey is his dedication to honoring his brothers' memories and their musical talents.

6. Natural Love:

Barry Gibb is well-known for his vast Miami, Florida property holdings and his love of the outdoors. He has participated in campaigns to save natural areas since he has a strong desire to preserve the environment.

7. Generosity:

Barry Gibb has supported causes about healthcare and music education through his charitable activities. His wish to have a positive influence outside of the music industry is shown in his dedication to giving back.

8. Acknowledgments and Awards:

Barry Gibb has won accolades for his musical accomplishments in addition to being named a 2004 Commander of the Order of the British Empire (CBE).

9. Individual Assists:

Barry Gibb's solo career, which consists of solo albums and sporadic live appearances, demonstrates his continuous love of music outside of the Bee Gees' group endeavors.

10. Concluding Our Musical Investigation:

Barry Gibb has persisted in pursuing new musical endeavors, evolving his approach while maintaining the core of the Bee Gees' sound. His solo endeavors, such as the 2016 album "In the Now," show his continued dedication to creative expression.

Barry Gibb

Barry Gibb's life story is characterized by strong ties to his family, perseverance in the face of hardship, and a profound love of music. His dedication to upholding the Bee Gees' legacy and supporting charitable endeavors demonstrates the depth of both his personal and professional life.

4.1 Legacy

Barry Gibb left behind a rich legacy that includes his significant influence on the music business, his important part in the Bee Gees, and his continuing effect on upcoming musical generations. This is a thorough analysis of Barry Gibb's legacy:

1. Originality in Music:

Barry Gibb, his brothers Maurice and Robin, and others were trailblazers in creating the sound of popular music. The Bee Gees' inventive approach to songwriting and harmonies left an enduring impression on the business, from their early days of experimenting with many genres to their domination throughout the disco era.

2. Mastery of Songwriting:

Barry Gibb's legacy is mostly based on his skill as a songwriter. His ability to write moving lyrics and timeless songs has added to the Bee Gees catalog's ongoing success. From ballads to disco anthems, many of their classics are still popular with listeners of all ages.

3. The Cultural Influence of Bee Gees:

During the disco era, The Bee Gees had an unmatched influence on popular culture, particularly with the music of "Saturday Night Fever". Their music not only came to define a time, but it also had an impact on dancing, fashion, and the late 1970s cultural environment as a whole.

4. Flexibility Throughout Genres:

Barry Gibb's ability to develop and perform a wide range of musical styles made it possible for the Bee Gees to move fluidly between genres. Their inventiveness while preserving a unique sound demonstrates Barry's versatility and inventiveness.

5. Enduring Chart Success:

Under Barry Gibb's direction, the Bee Gees recorded numerous number-one hits and albums, and they enjoyed extraordinary chart success. Their enduring appeal is further highlighted by their durability and consistency in the music industry.

6. Classic Falsetto Voices:

The falsetto vocals of Barry Gibb came to characterize the Bee Gees' sound. His strong and passionate voice is a defining feature of the group's career and helped shape their sound character.

7. Acknowledgment and Honours: Barry Gibb's countless honors, such as Grammys, Brit Awards, and admission into the Rock and Roll Hall of Fame, attest to his and the Bee Gees' enduring influence on the music business.

8. Resurgence of Culture:

In the late 1990s and early 2000s, The Bee Gees saw a rise in popularity as a result of their music being included in films and advertisements as well as a revived recognition of its historical significance in the music industry.

9. Donations to Charities:

Another aspect of Barry Gibb's legacy is his philanthropic support of issues like healthcare and music education, which demonstrates his dedication to leaving a constructive legacy outside of the music industry.

10. Source of Insight for Upcoming Artists:

Barry Gibb

Barry Gibb has influenced many performers in many genres, and his impact lives on. His impact can be heard in the works of musicians who value the Bee Gees' ageless sound.

Barry Gibb left behind a legacy of musical genius, tenacity, and inventiveness. His talents as a singer, songwriter, and cultural icon are still relevant today, guaranteeing that the Bee Gees' legacy will always be a noteworthy period in the history of popular music.

4.2 Discography

The discography of Barry Gibb includes both his solo endeavors and his time spent with the Bee Gees. A thorough examination of Barry Gibb's discography may be found here:

Alongside the Bee Gees:

The first studio album by the Bee Gees, released in 1967, had classics including "To Love Somebody" and "New York Mining Disaster 1941."

Horizontal (1968): The Bee Gees' continued experimentation with different musical genres was showcased on this album.

Barry Gibb

Idea (1968): The timeless song "I Started a Joke" was featured on the third album.

Odessa (1969): A concept album that showcased the wide range of musical influences that the Bee Gees had.

2. Disco Era:

Cucumber Castle (1970): The debut album follows Robin Gibb, delving into elements from both country and rock music.

2 Years Later (1970): The debut album with Barry and Maurice as a duo, including the popular song "Lonely Days."

In 1971, Trafalgar: Songs like "Don't Wanna Live Inside Me" and "How Can You Mend a Broken Heart" were on the CD.

To Whom It May Concern (1972): Included the popular song "Run to Me."

3. Mainstream Success:

Life in a Tin Can (1973): The Bee Gees went through a transitional era.

Barry Gibb

Mr. Natural (1974): had a sound that was more R&B-focused.

The seminal album Main Course (1975) introduced a funk and R&B vibe with singles like "Jive Talkin'."

Children of the World (1976): included the disco hit song "You Should Be Dancing."

4. The dominance of the Disco Era:

Spirits Having Flown (1979): At the height of the disco era, this album was enormously successful and included classics like "Tragedy" and "Too Much Heaven."

Discography Only:

Barry Gibb's first solo album, Flowing Rivers (1977), featured the popular song "I Just Want to Be Your Everything."

Shadow Dancing (1980): The popular title tune and additional tracks from the second solo album.

Barry's flexibility was on display with his more rock-oriented album Now Voyager (1984).

In the Now (2016): His first new solo album in over 30 years, fusing aspects of the old with the modern.

Barry Gibb

2. Collaborative Albums:

Guilty (1980): A very popular joint album with Barbra Streisand that included singles like "What Kind of Fool" and "Guilty."

Eyes That See in the Dark (1983): Kenny Rogers and the artist collaborated on an album that featured the popular song "Islands in the Stream."

3. Live and Compilation Albums: Barry Gibb Live (1989): Concert recording featuring Bee Gees and solo hits performed live.

Mythology (2010): A boxed compilation of Andy Gibb, Barry, Robin, and Maurice's music.

Barry Gibb's discography is a multi-decade journey through music that demonstrates his growth as a composer and performer. Every record, from the Bee Gees' earliest days to his solo projects, adds to the legacy of one of the most important figures in music history.

CHAPTER 5: COLLABORATIONS

Collaborations by Barry Gibb go beyond his work with his Bee Gees siblings. His flexibility as a musician and songwriter is demonstrated by the range of performers with whom he has worked. This is a thorough analysis of Barry Gibb's partnerships:

1.Barbra Streisand:

"Guilty" (1980) Collaborative Album: The album "Guilty," which Barry Gibb and Barbra Streisand collaborated on, was an enormous success. Hits like "What Kind of Fool" and the title tune showcased the rapport between the two legendary musicians.

2. The collaborative album "Eyes That See in the Dark" (1983) by Kenny Rogers: Kenny Rogers recorded an album with Barry Gibb producing and writing songs, including the timeless duet "Islands in the Stream."

3. "Heartbreaker" (1982) by Dionne Warwick: "Heartbreaker," the lead single from Dionne Warwick's album, was written and produced by

Barry Gibb

Barry Gibb, who also helped make the song popular.

4. Dion, Kenny, Barry, Streisand (SDKB):

Benefit Concert (1983): To raise money for charity, Barry Gibb collaborated with Barbra Streisand, Dionne Warwick, and Kenny Rogers on a benefit concert.

5. Olivia Newton-John:

"Face to Face" (1984): Olivia Newton-John and Barry Gibb worked together on the duet "Face to Face," which can be heard on Newton-John's album "Soul Kiss."

6. "Ebony and Ivory" (1982):

Paul McCartney: Barry Gibb was involved in the writing and production of the Paul McCartney and Stevie Wonder duet "Ebony and Ivory," demonstrating his impact in creating singles that reached the top of the charts even though it was not a direct collaboration.

7. "Make You Feel My Love" (2002) by Willie Nelson: A version of "Make You Feel My Love" by Bob Dylan with vocals by Barry Gibb was featured on Willie Nelson's CD "The Great Divide."

8. Sheryl Crow (2002):

"Run": Barry Gibb and Sheryl Crow co-wrote the song "Run," which can be found on Crow's album "C'mon, C'mon."

9. Barbra Streisand's "Encore: Movie Partners Sing Broadway" (2016): Barry Gibb co-starred with Barbra Streisand on the song "I Still Can See Your Face," which was included on Streisand's album of joint efforts.

10. "Words" (2017) by Dolly Parton: Barry Gibb and Dolly Parton worked together on the lead single from Gibb's solo album "Words," uniting two of the most recognizable voices in music.

Collaborations with a variety of musicians and genres demonstrate Barry Gibb's versatility. These partnerships which include writing songs, producing albums, and sharing the stage showcase Barry Gibb's talent and his ongoing impact on the music business.

5.1 Other Artists

Barry Gibb's impact goes beyond his Bee Gees days, as seen by his partnerships and contributions to other musicians. This is a thorough examination of Barry Gibb's collaborations with various artists:

1. "Guilty" (1980) Collaboration - Barbra Streisand: Barbra Streisand's album "Guilty" was produced and co-written by Barry Gibb. Hits like "What Kind of Fool" and the title track demonstrated the two musicians' connection.

2. The collaboration of Kenny Rogers with "Eyes That See in the Dark" (1983): Kenny Rogers' album featured songs written and produced by Barry Gibb, including the duet "Islands in the Stream," which went on to become a country-pop classic.

3. "Heartbreaker" (1982) by Dionne Warwick: "Heartbreaker," the lead single from Dionne Warwick's album, was written and produced by Barry Gibb, who also helped make the song popular.

4. Dion, Kenny, Barry, Streisand (SDKB):

Benefit Concert (1983): To support philanthropic organizations, Barry Gibb collaborated with Barbra Streisand, Dionne Warwick, and Kenny Rogers on a benefit event.

5. Olivia Newton-John:

"Face to Face" (1984): Olivia Newton-John and Barry Gibb worked together on the duet "Face to Face," which can be found on her album "Soul Kiss."

"Ebony and Ivory" (1982):

Paul McCartney: Barry Gibb's contribution as a songwriter can be seen in the Paul McCartney and Stevie Wonder duet "Ebony and Ivory," but it was not a direct collaboration.

7. "Make You Feel My Love" (2002) by Willie Nelson: A version of "Make You Feel My Love" by Bob Dylan with vocals by Barry Gibb was featured on Willie Nelson's CD "The Great Divide."

8. Sheryl Crow (2002):

"Run": Barry Gibb and Sheryl Crow co-wrote the song "Run," which can be found on Crow's album "C'mon, C'mon."

9. Barbra Streisand's "Encore: Movie Partners Sing Broadway" (2016):

Barry Gibb co-starred with Barbra Streisand on the song "I Still Can See Your Face," which was included on Streisand's album of joint efforts.

10. "Words" (2017) by Dolly Parton: Barry Gibb and Dolly Parton worked together on the lead single from Gibb's solo album "Words," uniting two of the most recognizable voices in music.

Barry Gibb's versatility and adaptability across a range of genres are demonstrated through his collaborations with other musicians. These varied collaborations demonstrate his influence on the larger musical scene, regardless of whether he is working as a songwriter, producer, or performer.

5.2 Film

Barry Gibb has been involved in several cinematic projects as of my last information update in January 2022; these projects have mostly to do with the Bee Gees soundtrack contributions and music. Please be aware that since then, there might have been more advancements or initiatives. This is a thorough analysis of Barry Gibb's cinematic work:

1. The 1977 film "Saturday Night Fever": In this classic movie, Barry Gibb and the Bee Gees were essential to the soundtrack. Numerous Bee Gees classics, such as "Stayin' Alive," "How Deep Is Your Love," and "Night Fever," were included on the soundtrack. The movie and its music have come to represent the disco era.

2. Releasing "Grease" in 1978: The Bee Gees contributed to the soundtrack of the movie "Grease," which starred Olivia Newton-John and John Travolta, but it was unrelated to Barry Gibb. Frankie Valli sang the Bee Gees song "Grease" in the movie.

3. "Sgt. Pepper's Lonely Hearts Club Band" (1978): Barry Gibb collaborated with several musicians on the musical film version of The Beatles' record "Sgt. Pepper's Lonely Hearts Club Band." In the movie, The Bee Gees played a fictional band and made musical contributions.

4. "Hawks" (1988): Barry Gibb wrote the soundtrack for Robert Ellis Miller's picture "Hawks." Timothy Dalton and Anthony Edwards starred in the movie, which follows a musician who must make a decision that could change his life.

5. "The Mini-Munsters" (1973): Barry Gibb and the Bee Gees appeared in a segment of "The Mini-Munsters." The Bee Gees sang their hits and had fun with the Munster family in this TV special.

6. The 2010 film "In Our Own Time": "In Our Own Time" is a documentary on the career of the Bee Gees, albeit not a traditional movie. In addition to interviewing and showing archive material, Barry

Gibb and the band's then-surviving members, Robin and Maurice, talked about the band's past.

7. In 2020, "How Can You Mend a Broken Heart": "How Can You Mend a Broken Heart" is a Frank Marshall-directed documentary that follows the Bee Gees' career, delving into their ascent to fame, the difficulties they encountered, and their enduring influence on the music business. There are several interviews and insights with Barry Gibb.

Barry Gibb's cinematic career is intimately linked to the Bee Gees' music and their noteworthy inclusions on numerous soundtracks. His influence on the film industry is still entwined with the Bee Gees' musical journey, whether it is through classic disco-era movies or documentaries delving into the band's history.

5.3 Television

Over his career, Barry Gibb has been involved with television through a range of performances, appearances, and show contributions. This is a thorough analysis of Barry Gibb's television appearances:

1. A Variety of TV Appearances: Barry Gibb and the Bee Gees performed on talk shows, variety shows,

and music specials on television multiple times over the years. Their performances, conversations, and interactions with hosts were all on display throughout these engagements.

2. "The Ed Sullivan Show": The Bee Gees performed some of their early songs and gained exposure to a large television audience during their several appearances on "The Ed Sullivan Show" in the 1960s.

3. "Saturday Night Live" (SNL): The Bee Gees made multiple appearances on "Saturday Night Live," appearing in memorable sketches and playing their singles. During the musical segments of the show, the band frequently demonstrated their variety.

4. "Solid Gold" (1981): Barry Gibb sang his solo smash song "Guilty" during a solo appearance on the music variety show "Solid Gold."

5. "The Tonight Show Starring Johnny Carson": The Bee Gees, with Barry Gibb, performed and conducted interviews on "The Tonight Show" on several occasions while Johnny Carson was host.

6. "Oprah Winfrey Show": Barry Gibb and the Bee Gees made an appearance on "The Oprah Winfrey

Show," where they talked about their personal and professional life as well as the influence of their music.

7. "Late Night with Jimmy Fallon": In 2013, Barry Gibb took part in an iconic sketch on "Late Night with Jimmy Fallon" in which he and Fallon, who was portraying Barry, did a fictitious interview and sang a rendition of "Jive Talkin'" with the iconic falsetto of the Bee Gees.

8. "Glastonbury Festival" (2017): In 2017, Barry Gibb was the main attraction on the Pyramid Stage of the Glastonbury Festival. He gave a powerful performance that was shown on television and demonstrated his enduring stage presence.

9.The 2017 film "Stayin' Alive: A Grammy Salute to the Music of the Bee Gees": A TV show honoring Barry Gibb, the Bee Gees, and their contribution to the music business. A homage to the Bee Gees was performed by a variety of artists during the event.

10. Specials and Documentaries: Several films and specials about the Bee Gees and Barry Gibb's career have included him. Among the most notable is the HBO documentary "How Can You Mend a

Barry Gibb

Broken Heart" (2020), which offers a detailed look at the Bee Gees' life story.

Barry Gibb has had a varied television career, appearing in interviews, variety shows, and classic music shows. His television appearances, whether with the Bee Gees or on his own, have been crucial to the band's popularity and heritage.

CHAPTER 6: CHALLENGES

Barry Gibb has had tremendous success in the music business, but he has also had to overcome many obstacles in his life and profession. Here is a thorough analysis of some of the difficulties Barry Gibb has faced:

1. Brothers' Loss: The deaths of his younger brothers, Andy Gibb in 1988, Maurice Gibb in 2003, and Robin Gibb in 2012, were among the biggest setbacks for Barry Gibb. These setbacks signaled the end of an era for the Bee Gees and had a significant personal and professional influence on Barry.

2. The Shifting Musical Terrain: Like many other musicians, the Bee Gees had to adjust to changes in the music business. Following the disco era's enormous success, they had difficulty keeping up with changing public tastes and musical trends.

3. Views and Reactions from the Public: The Bee Gees faced criticism and backlash in the late 1970s during the anti-discrimination movement. The Bee Gees' tightly linked genre saw a drop in popularity, which made it difficult for them to retain their public persona.

4. Health Concerns: Barry Gibb has experienced health concerns at various times in his life. Nevertheless, he has persisted and kept up an active profession despite these obstacles.

5. Bereavement and Emotional Challenges: For Barry Gibb, the death of close relatives especially his brothers was a contributing factor in his sad moments and emotional challenges. Resilience was needed to deal with these losses and carry on creating and performing.

6. Changing Trends in Music: For any artist with a lengthy career, it can be difficult to adjust to shifting musical trends. The Bee Gees had to modify their strategy to remain relevant as popular music trends changed from the disco era to later decades.

7. Solo Career Transition: Following the Bee Gees era, Barry Gibb encountered difficulties in pursuing a solo career. To forge an independent identity apart from the recognizable group dynamic, he had to overcome preconceptions and demonstrate his abilities as a solo artist.

8. Handling Notoriety: It might be difficult to deal with the pressures that come with fame. The Bee Gees had to deal with the pressures of international fame, media criticism, and public expectations,

particularly during the disco era when they were at their height.

9. Creative Development: Barry Gibb had to balance his creative growth as a songwriter and guitarist with maintaining the core of the Bee Gees' sound. It required ongoing artistic adaptation to strike a balance between innovation and preserving their distinctive style.

10. Perseverance in the Industry: Over the years, maintaining creative integrity, being relevant, and navigating the ever-changing music industry are problems that will never go away. Barry Gibb's tenacity in the face of changes in the music industry is evidence of his dedication to the genre.

Despite these difficulties, Barry Gibb's lasting legacy is a testament to his fortitude in the face of both personal and professional adversity as well as his capacity to overcome hurdles. His career path in the music business is a tribute to the challenges and successes of a lifetime of work.

6.1 Triumphs

Many victories throughout his life and career have demonstrated Barry Gibb's tenacity, inventiveness, and long-lasting influence on the music business.

Barry Gibb

This is a thorough analysis of Barry Gibb's achievements:

1. Worldwide Chart Domination: The Bee Gees, led by Barry, had a run of number-one hits that topped the charts for several decades, helping them to unprecedented success. In the annals of popular music, their ability to rule the charts worldwide from the 1960s to the 2000s is an accomplishment.

2. Iconic Songwriting: Barry Gibb's compositional abilities were essential to the Bee Gees' triumph. His ability to write timeless and varied songs in a wide range of genres from disco anthems to ballads established the Bee Gees as one of the finest songwriting teams in the history of music.

3. The soundtrack of "Saturday Night Fever": The Bee Gees' triumphant contribution to the soundtrack of "Saturday Night Fever" is timeless. The record won the Grammy Awards and received praise from all around the world in addition to becoming one of the best-selling soundtracks and defining the disco period.

4. Adaptability in the Face of Opposition: The Bee Gees encountered opposition during the anti-disco movement in the late 1970s. They showed tenacity by changing their sound, releasing hits, and leaving

a lasting impression in the face of criticism and a brief drop in popularity.

5. Induction into the Songwriters Hall of Fame: In 1994, Barry Gibb and his siblings were admitted into the Songwriters Hall of Fame. This accolade confirms their place in music history and acknowledges their outstanding contribution to the craft of songwriting.

6. Grammy Awards: Barry Gibb won multiple Grammy Awards with the Bee Gees, including Best Pop Performance by a Duo or Group with Vocal, Record of the Year, and Album of the Year.

7. Rock & Roll Hall of Fame: In 1997, The Bee Gees, which included Barry Gibb, were inducted into the hall to honor their continuing impact on the development of popular music.

8. Guinness World Records: The Guinness World Records now includes Barry Gibb and the Bee Gees as the group with the most consecutive Hot 100 number-one hits in the United States, a stellar achievement in the chart sphere.

9. Success in Solo Career: Barry Gibb's solo endeavors, which include hit albums like "Flowing Rivers," "Guilty," and "In the Now," demonstrate his

ability to sustain a prosperous career after the Bee Gees heyday.

10. Legacy and Persuasion: Beyond his life, Barry Gibb's accomplishments as a songwriter, performer, and important member of the Bee Gees will live on. The Bee Gees' long-lasting success in the music industry is demonstrated by the music's continuing impact on later generations of musicians and the larger cultural environment.

Barry Gibb's victories are a reflection of the Bee Gees' group success as well as his accomplishments. In the annals of popular music history, their influence on the music industry, spanning decades and genres, continues to be an enduring accomplishment.

6.2 Peaks

Barry Gibb's life and career have been filled with highs and lows, remarkable achievements and difficult times. This is a thorough examination of Barry Gibb's journey's highs and lows:

High points:

1. The Bee Gees' Worldwide Success: The Bee Gees' international triumph was one of the

highlights of Barry Gibb's career. The Bee Gees ruled charts all over the world from the 1960s to the 2000s, racking up incredible success with hits in many different genres.

2. The soundtrack of "Saturday Night Fever": The Bee Gees' song from "Saturday Night Fever" is the highlight of their career. The record characterized the disco period and went on to become a global sensation in addition to winning several Grammy Awards.

3. creative Brilliance: Highlights of Barry Gibb's career include his hit songs "How Deep Is Your Love" and "Stayin' Alive," which demonstrate his creative prowess. His ability to write songs that were both timeless and varied added to the Bee Gees' enduring influence.

4. Induction into the Rock & Roll Hall of Fame: In 1997, the Bee Gees, which included Barry Gibb, were honored with a seat in the Hall, acknowledging their significant impact on the music business.

5. Grammy Awards: The Bee Gees were honored with several Grammy Awards, including top honors like Record of the Year and Album of the Year.

Barry Gibb

These honors demonstrate their industry recognition and superior musical ability.

6. Success in Solo Career: Barry Gibb's solo career, which included hit albums like "In the Now" and "Flowing Rivers," is a high point. His adaptability is demonstrated by his ability to succeed as a solo artist.

7. Cultural Impact and Legacy: The peak of Barry Gibb's career was the cultural effect and legacy of The Bee Gees. Their lasting appeal and impact on later musical generations highlight their importance in the annals of music history.

lows

1. Younger Brothers' Loss: The passing of Barry Gibb's younger brothers, Andy in 1988, Maurice in 2003, and Robin in 2012, was one of the hardest low points of his life. Barry was greatly affected by these setbacks on a personal and professional level.

2. Opposition and Criticism: In the late 1970s, amid the anti-disco movement, The Bee Gees encountered opposition and criticism. The Bee Gees' public image was impacted by the genre's

loss in popularity, which was strongly linked to them.

3. Shifting Musical Trends: It was difficult to adjust to the ever-evolving musical trends. Following the disco period, The Bee Gees had to adapt to changes in popular music trends to remain relevant.

4. Fall in Adolescent Attraction: A low point was the Bee Gees' loss in popularity following the disco era. It was difficult to navigate shifts in public opinion and musical tastes.

5. Handling Loss: Barry Gibb struggled to deal with his brothers' deaths on an emotional level and experienced grief. It took strength and resiliency to go over these terrible points in one's life.

6. Health Challenges: Barry Gibb has experienced health issues that have affected his well-being at various times throughout his life. Taking care of health problems is a low point for you.

7. Public criticism: The Bee Gees faced difficult times navigating shifting perceptions due to public criticism, particularly during the disco heyday and the ensuing decline in popularity.

The ups and downs of Barry Gibb's life and career have reflected the complexity of a lengthy and

Barry Gibb

influential musical legacy. Notwithstanding the difficulties, his accomplishments and enduring contributions cemented his place in popular music history.

CHAPTER 7: RESILIENCE IN THE INDUSTRY

One of the things that has defined Barry Gibb's career in the music business is his tenacity. He has exhibited strength, resilience, and an unrelenting commitment to his profession while overcoming many obstacles and changes in the music industry. This is a thorough examination of Barry Gibb's fortitude:

1. Flexibility in Response to Shifting Musical Trends: Barry Gibb demonstrated adaptability in response to shifting musical trends. He moved through several genres and styles following the disco backlash of the late 1970s, making sure the Bee Gees remained relevant in the business.

2. Success in the Post-Disco Era: After disco faded, Barry Gibb and the Bee Gees proved resilient, succeeding in the decades that followed with singles like "One" and "Alone." Their adaptability to changing musical tastes was demonstrated by their ability to reimagine their sound.

Barry Gibb

3. Solo Career Transition: Barry Gibb showed resiliency by leaving the Bee Gees' group dynamic and embarking on a solo career. "Flowing Rivers" and "In the Now," two of his solo albums, demonstrated his unique talent and tenacity in sustaining a prosperous solo career.

4. Managing Bereavement: The demise of his brothers, Robin and Maurice Gibb, presented significant obstacles on both a personal and professional level. Barry Gibb's ability to bounce back from these losses was demonstrated by his ability to make music, respect their legacy, and deal with his emotions.

5. Adhering to the Tradition of Songwriting: Barry Gibb never wavered from his songwriter roots during his career. His dedication to writing timeless melodies demonstrated his ability to uphold his artistic integrity in the face of changes in the music business.

6. Philanthropic Contributions: Barry Gibb's philanthropic work, which includes funding for healthcare and music education, shows tenacity outside of the music business. His tenacity in meeting larger societal demands is demonstrated by his dedication to having a good influence.

7. Return to the Stage: Barry Gibb showed tenacity and an unwavering love for live music despite the difficulties associated with performing and touring as he made his way back to the stage, performing at important occasions like the Glastonbury Festival.

8. Cultural Resurgence: In the late 1990s and early 2000s, The Bee Gees saw a rise in popularity. Barry Gibb's tenacity was demonstrated when their music was used in movies and advertisements and received fresh attention, enhancing its influence on listeners of all ages.

9. Artistic Exploration: Barry Gibb's desire to work with musicians from other genres and experiment with diverse musical approaches is a testament to his tenacity. His willingness to experiment with art demonstrates his ability to change with the times without losing his unique style.

10. "How Can You Mend a Broken Heart" Documentary: Barry Gibb's involvement in the 2020 Bee Gees documentary, "How Can You Mend a Broken Heart," showed tenacity in reflecting on the highs and lows of their career and offered insights into their path and legacy.

In addition to his ability to persevere in the face of adversity, Barry Gibb's resilience in the music business is demonstrated by his constant innovation, adaptation, and contribution to the dynamic field of popular music. His outstanding career is defined by strength and drive, which are evidenced by his enduring legacy.

7.1 Impact on Musical Industry

Barry Gibb has had a significant and wide-ranging influence on music over many decades and genres. Both as a solo artist and as a pivotal member of the Bee Gees, his talents have made a lasting impression on the music business. This is a thorough examination of Barry Gibb's influence on music:

1. Pioneering Songwriting: Barry Gibb, together with his brothers Robin and Maurice, established a unique songwriting style distinguished by complex melodies, nuanced emotional content, and moving lyrics. Their talent to write classic tunes had a profound effect on songwriting.

2. The Vocal Harmony of the Bee Gees: The Bee Gees' distinctive three-part harmony, which frequently included Barry's falsetto, became well-known and added to their distinctive sound. They

stood out from the crowd with their vocal arrangements, which impacted many musicians from all genres.

3. Dominance of the Disco period: Barry Gibb's Bee Gees were instrumental in creating the sound of the disco period. Popular songs like "How Deep Is Your Love" and "Stayin' Alive" cemented their influence on popular culture by becoming anthems of the era in addition to topping charts.

4. "Saturday Night Fever" Soundtrack: The Bee Gees' songs from the soundtrack, such as "Stayin' Alive," "How Deep Is Your Love," and "Night Fever," not only helped to define the disco genre but also went on to become some of the most well-known and best-selling tracks in music history.

5. Flexibility Throughout Genres: The Bee Gees' ability to experiment with many genres is a testament to Barry Gibb's versatility as a songwriter and performer. They were able to move between pop, rock, R&B, and disco with ease, demonstrating their influence over a wide range of musical genres.

6. tunes and Legacy: Under Barry's direction, the Bee Gees have a wealth of timeless tunes in their repertoire. Their songs are still acclaimed, covered,

and sampled, leaving a lasting impression on musicians of later generations.

7. Collaboration with Other Artists: A varied musical legacy has resulted from Barry Gibb's collaborations with performers such as Barbra Streisand, Kenny Rogers, Dolly Parton, and others. These partnerships demonstrate his versatility and capacity to contribute significantly outside of the Bee Gees.

8. Persistent Solo Success: Barry Gibb's solo career, which includes albums like "In the Now" and "Flowing Rivers," exemplifies his ongoing influence as a solo artist. His solo projects demonstrate his ongoing capacity to write interesting and timely music.

9. Impact on Vocal Design: Barry Gibb's unique vocal style which is distinguished by his falsetto range has impacted musicians in later generations. His passionate and expressive vocal approach has served as an inspiration to other artists from various genres.

10. Influence on Culture and Film: The Bee Gees' music has influenced popular culture and film, particularly during the "Saturday Night Fever" era. Numerous movies have included their music,

resulting in memorable moments and influencing culture.

Barry Gibb's influence on music goes beyond his position on the charts. His ability to adapt, write inventive songs, and sing have solidified his status as a musical legend. He has influenced musicians from many genres and left a lasting legacy in the annals of popular music.

7.2 Influence on Genres

Barry Gibb's impact on music is multifaceted, demonstrating his adaptability and influence on the changing face of popular music. This is a thorough examination of Barry Gibb's impact on several genres:

1. Pop Music: Barry Gibb has made a huge impact on pop music. He was a key figure in creating the pop sound of the 1960s and beyond as the lead vocalist and songwriter for the Bee Gees. Pop music has evolved substantially as a result of The Bee Gees' ability to write memorable melodies and poignant lyrics.

2. Disco: Barry Gibb's Bee Gees became a household name throughout the disco period. Not only did their contributions to the soundtrack of

Barry Gibb

"Saturday Night Fever" include classics like "Stayin' Alive" and "Night Fever," but they also helped to define disco and brought the genre-wide recognition. Barry's falsetto voice turned became a signature sound in disco music.

3. Soul and R&B: The Bee Gees' experimentation with R&B and soul components demonstrated Barry Gibb's versatility in blending many inspirations. Contributing to the R&B genre, songs like "How Deep Is Your Love" and "Love So Right" showed off their mastery of soulful melodies and rhythms.

4. Soft Rock: The songwriting approach of Barry Gibb was a perfect fit for the soft rock genre. Hits like "How Can You Mend a Broken Heart" and "I Started a Joke" by the Bee Gees demonstrated their talent for writing emotionally charged soft rock ballads, which impacted subsequent musicians in the genre.

5. Country Music: Barry Gibb's contributions to country music are evident through his partnerships with performers such as Dolly Parton and Kenny Rogers. Songs like "Words" (with Dolly Parton) and "Islands in the Stream" (with Kenny Rogers) demonstrate his crossover success and influence on the country music genre.

6. Adult Contemporary: The gentler songs and ballads of The Bee Gees were a perfect fit for the adult contemporary genre. The group's harmonies and Barry Gibb's skill as a songwriter produced a collection of songs that appealed to adult contemporary audiences.

7. Rock music: Even though the Bee Gees are frequently linked to pop and disco, their early work had rock music influences. Barry Gibb's vocal flexibility gave the Bee Gees the freedom to experiment with many rock genre features, resulting in a wide range of musical styles.

8. Pop-Dance: Barry Gibb's influence on dance-pop persisted even after the disco period. Dance-pop artists of later generations owe a debt of gratitude to The Bee Gees for their addictive rhythms and danceable beats.

9. Spiritual and Gospel Music: Particularly in his later years, Barry Gibb's solo endeavors have incorporated aspects of spiritual and gospel music. His investigation of topics with a more profound spiritual resonance demonstrates his ability to include a variety of components in his musical repertory.

Barry Gibb

10. Contemporary Collaborations: Barry Gibb's openness to working with modern musicians shows how much of an impact he still has on contemporary music. His ability to relate to new generations of musicians and audiences is demonstrated by his collaborations with performers from many genres.

Barry Gibb's effect on genres transcends style borders, a testament to his versatility and enduring power. His musical talents, which range from disco anthems to heartfelt ballads, have irrevocably altered the wide range of popular music genres.

CHAPTER 8: CULTURAL SIGNIFICANCE

The cultural impact of Barry Gibb goes well beyond his accomplishments as a singer, composer, and Bee Gees member. He has had a profound cultural influence and left a lasting legacy that spans decades. A thorough examination of Barry Gibb's cultural relevance can be found here:

1. Icon of the Disco Era: Barry Gibb, the lead vocalist of the Bee Gees, was instrumental in creating the disco era's distinctive sound. During the late 1970s, the Bee Gees' contributions to the "Saturday Night Fever" soundtrack evolved into disco movement anthems that influenced dancing, fashion, and popular culture.

2. A Generation's Soundtrack: The disco period of The Bee Gees' music in particular became a generation's soundtrack. In addition to topping charts, hits like "Stayin' Alive" and "How Deep Is Your Love" captured the zeitgeist and vigor of the era.

3. Influence on Fashion: The Bee Gees' unique look, which included flowing hair, open-collar shirts, and sleek suits, enhanced the aesthetics of 1970s fashion. Their impact on style trends turned into a

fundamental component of the zeitgeist of the culture.

4. The phenomenon known as "Saturday Night Fever": A cultural phenomenon resulted from the popularity of the "Saturday Night Fever" movie and music, in which Barry Gibb had a big part. The Bee Gees' music and the film's depiction of the disco lifestyle influenced popular culture and changed the entertainment industry.

5. Resurgence in the years 2000 and 1990: The Bee Gees saw a comeback in the 1990s and early 2000s as a result of its classic songs being used in TV shows, advertising, and motion pictures. Its music was made accessible to new audiences during this comeback, which added to its long-lasting cultural influence.

6. Effect on Dance and Choreography: The catchy beats and danceable rhythms of The Bee Gees' music had an impact on dance and choreography. The signature moves linked with Bee Gees songs were seen at discotheques and dance floors worldwide, influencing dance culture.

7. Cultural Allusions in Cinema and TV: The Bee Gees' music has been heavily included in several TV series and movies, being associated with

specific moments and times. Their songs emphasize their enduring influence by frequently acting as cultural markers in narratives.

8. Enduring Cross-Generational Appeal: The Bee Gees' appeal to a wide age range contributes to the cultural relevance of Barry Gibb. Their music is still in high demand among listeners of all ages, proving its enduring value and cultural significance.

9. Cultural Plundering in Remix Songs: Many musicians from a variety of genres have honored the Bee Gees with cover songs. This cross-cultural interaction illustrates how Barry Gibb's lyrics and the Bee Gees' musical legacy continue to influence modern musicians.

10. Cultural Archivist: Barry Gibb has documented the Bee Gees' journey through films, interviews, and personal works. His thoughts and observations support the preservation of the band's cultural heritage and influence on the music business.

Barry Gibb's cultural relevance stems from his important role in forming musical genres, fashion, and the collective recollections of many eras. His influence endures, cementing his place in popular culture from the disco era to current cultural allusions.

8.1 Philanthropy

Throughout his life, Barry Gibb has been actively involved in philanthropy, supporting a range of projects that demonstrate his dedication to having a beneficial impact on society. This is a thorough analysis of Barry Gibb's charitable pursuits:

1. Music Education: Barry Gibb has promoted music education vigorously. He understands the value of sponsoring school music programs and giving aspiring artists opportunities. His efforts are intended to develop the musical talent of the upcoming generation.

2. Healthcare efforts: Barry Gibb has made contributions to healthcare efforts that center on the diagnosis, diagnosis, and treatment of a range of medical ailments. His backing of healthcare institutions demonstrates his commitment to tackling medical issues and enhancing health results.

3. Environmental Conservation: Barry Gibb has always placed a high value on environmental issues. His support of conservation initiatives shows that he is dedicated to protecting the environment and spreading knowledge about the value of sustainable practices.

4. Assistance for Disasters: Barry Gibb has demonstrated a commitment to helping impacted areas after natural catastrophes. His charitable endeavors in disaster relief demonstrate his sympathy for those going through difficult times and his readiness to help in the healing process.

5. Generous Activities and Exhibitions: Barry Gibb frequently contributes his skills to performances and gatherings for charity. He uses his musical influence to make a difference, whether he's arranging events to raise money for charities or taking part in benefit concerts.

6. Awareness of Cancer: Barry Gibb has always had a deep passion for the causes of cancer research and awareness. His participation in cancer-related efforts shows a personal commitment to the problem, probably prompted by the deaths of his brothers Maurice and Robin.

7. philanthropic Efforts: Barry Gibb has participated in many philanthropic endeavors, giving to groups that address social concerns, advance education, and lessen poverty. His charitable endeavors include aiding more general humanitarian problems.

8. Community Development: To strengthen and empower communities, Barry Gibb has participated in community development projects. His charitable efforts go beyond international concerns to include projects that have a direct influence on nearby communities.

9. Working with Nonprofit Organizations: To maximize the impact of his donations, Barry Gibb has partnered with well-known nonprofits. His partnerships with respectable groups guarantee that his charity is focused on well-run, efficient projects, whether it be through financial support or awareness-raising.

10. Bequests and Tributaries: Barry Gibb's efforts to philanthropy will probably have a long-term effect on the issues he champions. Through consistent efforts and the advocacy of sustainable solutions, he guarantees that his philanthropy makes a lasting impact.

Barry Gibb's charitable endeavors demonstrate a strong sense of duty and empathy for other people's welfare. He has left a legacy that goes beyond his musical accomplishments by using his influence to bring about positive change through his donations to a variety of organizations.

8.2 Recent Projects

Barry Gibb was engaged in the following endeavors and pursuits at that period:

1.In 2021, "Greenfields: The Gibb Brothers Songbook, Vol. 1":

The CD "Greenfields: The Gibb Brothers Songbook, Vol. 1" was one of Barry Gibb's most important recent endeavors, and it was released in January 2021. Reimagined versions of beloved Bee Gees songs were included on the album, which also included collaborations with a variety of musicians from other genres, such as Sheryl Crow, Keith Urban, and Dolly Parton.

2. Headline Act for the 2020 Glastonbury Festival: The COVID-19 pandemic forced the cancellation of the 2020 Glastonbury Festival, which had Barry Gibb as the main act on the Pyramid Stage. As an homage, the festival's organizers aired a video from his prior appearance at Glastonbury in 2017.

3. The 2020 documentary "How Can You Mend a Broken Heart": In the December 2020 premiere of the documentary "How Can You Mend a Broken Heart," Barry Gibb took part. The HBO-produced documentary offers a thorough examination of the

Barry Gibb

Bee Gees' life story, musical influence, and difficulties.

4. Collaborations and Features: Barry Gibb is still involved in artistic collaborations. His involvement in a range of musical endeavors, appearances, and partnerships demonstrates his ongoing influence in the music business.

5. Solo Performances: Barry Gibb has occasionally taken the stage by himself, displaying his classic voice and charisma. He frequently performs solo, incorporating both Bee Gees classics and music from his albums.

6. Charitable Pursuits: Barry Gibb is well-known for his charitable endeavors. Even if some of his most recent endeavors might not have received much attention, he has probably continued to support many humanitarian causes, such as healthcare, music education, and disaster assistance.

7. Honors and Commemorative Events: Barry Gibb has received recognition and honors for his contributions to music. His recent actions include commemorative events, awards, and honors that recognize his lasting influence.

CHAPTER 9: QUOTES

Throughout his career, Barry Gibb, who is well-known for his work with the Bee Gees and other contributions to the music industry, has offered perceptive and thoughtful opinions. The following well-known statements by Barry Gibb provide insight into his outlook on life, music, and creativity:

1. On the Influence of Music: Music is the life-giving substance.

2. On Songwriting: Writing music is my way of expelling the devil from myself. It is akin to possessiveness. The tune prevents you from falling asleep even though you try.

3. Regarding Perseverance: We were consistently informed that 'You guys are going to make it.' But until now, I never thought that to be true. I believe that we are.

4. Regarding the Musical Style of the Bee Gees: We consider ourselves to be songwriters first and foremost. The Bee Gees are not so much a vocal quartet as they are a composing team.

5. Regarding Achievement and Criticism: Happiness is not correlated with success. The secret to success is happiness. You will succeed if you are passionate about what you are doing.

6. On Creativity: Every so often, I'll make a song that seems to come out of nowhere, and I don't know where it came from.

7. On the Legacy of the Bee Gees: We're not going to reinvent ourselves as the Bee Gees. All I want to do is keep writing and providing content.

8. On the Musical Journey: Music exhibits remarkable qualities. It can arouse emotions and sentiments in inexplicable ways.

9. **On the Musical Range of the Bee Gees** - "We can write and sing pretty songs, but we're not pretty people."

10. The Influence of "Saturday Night Fever": "A phenomenon occurred. It has become a phenomenon. It simply won't perish.

11. On Timelessness and Legacy: "I want music to last a lifetime. I want it to be a topic of discussion and listening for a very long time."

12. On the Difficulties in the Music Business: "The music industry is a strange combination of having real and intangible assets: pop bands are brand names.

Barry Gibb's love of music, commitment to writing songs, and opinions on creativity and success are all reflected in these quotations. His remarks shed light on the thoughts of a performer who has left a lasting impression on the music industry.

9.1 Fanbase

The generations-spanning devotion and diversity of Barry Gibb's fan base are a testament to the long-lasting influence of both his solo and Bee Gees career. This is a thorough analysis of Barry Gibb's fandom:

1. Appeal to Multiple Generations: Barry Gibb's fan base is surprisingly cross-generational, drawing in newer listeners who found his music in later decades together with longtime followers that date back to the Bee Gees' early 1960s days. The Bee Gees' catalog's timeless quality guarantees that their appeal is ageless.

2. Global Reach: Barry Gibb's music is heard all over the world, both as part of the Bee Gees and on

his own. His songs' universal themes and melodies draw in fans from all over the world, which helps to explain his wide-ranging and eclectic fan base.

3. Committed Online Communities: Social media groups, forums, and fan websites are just a few of the online spaces where Barry Gibb's followers congregate, exchange stories, talk music, and keep up to current on his most recent endeavors. These groups help followers who are passionate about their work to bond with one another.

4. Concert Attendance and Live Events: Fans go from all over the world to concert venues to see Barry Gibb perform live. A unique chance for fans to witness the enchantment of his music in person, these events feature solo performances or celebrations of the Bee Gees legacy.

5. Occasions Honoring and Reprise Artists: Fans frequently plan cover songs or tribute concerts to honor Barry Gibb's musical talents. These events highlight the inventiveness and passion of the fan base in honoring their favorite musician.

6. Music's Emotional Connection: Barry Gibb's music has a strong emotional bond with many of his admirers, who attest to the significant influence his songs have had on their lives. Barry's expressive

vocals, poignant lyrics, and stirring melodies all work together to create a deep bond between the performer and his fan base.

7. Expressions of gratitude for songwriting: Fans of Barry Gibb who have a deep respect for songwriting are not uncommon. His songs' deep lyrics, careful arrangements, and narrative components appeal to listeners who value the artistry of the music.

8. Assistance with Charity Pursuits: Supporters frequently agree with Barry Gibb's charitable pursuits. His dedication to issues like disaster assistance, healthcare, and music education strikes a chord with a fan base that also aspires to make a positive impact on society.

9. Honoring the Legacy of Barry Gibb: Supporters are deeply respectful of Barry Gibb's musical past in addition to his current work. Fans will always be able to appreciate and delve deeper into the complex fabric that the Bee Gees' lasting influence on the music business and Barry's accomplishments create.

10. Fan Engagement with Documentaries and Biographical Works: The fans of Barry Gibb actively participate in watching documentaries, reading

biographical pieces, and listening to interviews that offer insights into his personal and professional life. This curiosity is a reflection of a wish to learn more about the background information on the songs and the artist's life story.

The long bond Barry Gibb has built with listeners around the world and the timeless quality of his music is attested to by his devoted fan base. Through mutual experiences, in-person gatherings, or virtual exchanges, the fan community persistently commemorates and values Barry Gibb's musical heritage.

9.2 Tribute

A passionate celebration of the life, music, and legacy of the legendary singer is a Barry Gibb tribute. Barry Gibb's achievements in the music industry can be honored by fans, fellow musicians, and industry professionals through a variety of tributes, including live performances and commemorative events. A thorough examination of Barry Gibb tributes can be found here:

1. Live Events and Concerts: To honor Barry Gibb's musical legacy, tribute events often feature performers covering his songs. These concerts frequently feature a roster of gifted artists who

masterfully recreate solo successes and Bee Gees classics, encapsulating Barry Gibb's unique sound.

2. Commemorative Events: Fans and admirers can gather to honor Barry Gibb's legacy on occasions like the anniversaries of important career turning points or the Bee Gees' accomplishments. Documentary screenings, roundtable talks, and special performances are a few possible activities.

3. Homage Performances and Cover Songs: Songs by Barry Gibb are often included in concerts by musicians and bands as a way to honor his legacy and influence on music. These cover songs pay homage to Barry Gibb's musical prowess and vocal talent, whether they are performed live, on television, or online.

4. Biographical Writings and Documentaries: By detailing Barry Gibb's life story, musical career, and accomplishments in the music industry, documentaries and biographical works provide a thorough homage to the musician. These works offer a complex portrait of Barry Gibb's legacy through archive film, interviews, and comments from colleagues and family members.

5. Tributes on Social Media: Fans can post memories, messages of gratitude, and tributes to

Barry Gibb

Barry Gibb on social media platforms. Fan art, captioned images, and hashtags all add to the public's expression of appreciation and thanks for the singer.

6. Charitable and Fundraising Events: Barry Gibb tributes could perhaps act as a means of generating money for causes that are dear to his heart. These activities are in line with Barry Gibb's charitable endeavors and demonstrate a wish to pay tribute to his memory by giving back to the community.

7. Awards and Honors: Barry Gibb's accomplishments and contributions to music are frequently honored at awards ceremonies and honors. Honors such as lifetime achievement awards, inductions into the Hall of Fame, and other high-profile recognitions pay homage to his long-lasting influence on the music business.

8. Artistic Homages: Painters, sculptors, and multimedia installers are just a few of the ways that artists and makers honor Barry Gibb. These artistic tributes to Barry Gibb's lasting legacy encapsulate the essence of his persona, music, and cultural significance.

9. Collaborative Projects: Original music, movies, and multimedia experiences can honor Barry Gibb as part of collaborative projects with musicians, filmmakers, and other creatives. These initiatives provide fresh approaches to honor his legacy and investigate his long-lasting effects on music.

10. Legacy Preservation: The tributes paid to Barry Gibb are essential to keeping his legacy alive for upcoming generations. Through commemorating his musical contributions, highlighting his accomplishments, and narrating his life narrative, these tributes guarantee that Barry Gibb's impact will endure for an extended period.

Barry Gibb tributes are poignant ways to show appreciation, respect, and gratitude for a singer whose influence on culture and music is still incalculable. These tributes honor the eternal nature of Barry Gibb's songs and pay homage to his enduring legacy, whether through live performances, memorial services, or creative works.

Barry Gibb

CONCLUSION

As we come to the end of our examination of Barry Gibb's life and career, it is impossible not to be amazed by the remarkable trip taken by a musical legend. Barry Gibb's tale is one of perseverance, ingenuity, and unwavering devotion, spanning from his early years in Redcliffe, Australia, to his triumph as a solo artist and as the leader of the Bee Gees on the international stage.

The story has been told in chapters that have covered his early years, the Bee Gees' inception, their success during the disco period, and Barry's solo endeavors. His experiences, triumphant and difficult at times, weave a tapestry that depicts an artist who is not limited by genres in music.

The immense influence of songs like "Stayin' Alive" and "How Deep Is Your Love," along with the discography's wealth and signature falsetto vocals, make it clear that Barry Gibb has made an incalculable contribution to the arts. His skill as a songwriter and the harmonies that shaped the Bee Gees' style have left a lasting impression on numerous generations' soundtracks.

Barry Gibb

The final chapters have examined Barry Gibb's cultural significance, his charitable activities, and the variety of memorials that have been created to honor his legacy. Since Barry Gibb's influence can still be felt in the hearts of fans everywhere and in the works of contemporary artists, his story is not just a historical record but a live one.

Even after the last note is played, Barry Gibb's lasting influence can be found beyond a book's pages. It is evident in the songs that enthrall audiences time and time again, in the charitable endeavors that have a positive effect, and in the cultural relevance that endures.

The life of Barry Gibb is proof of the ability of music to raise, inspire, and unite people from all walks of life. This exploration's conclusion is not a sign of closure but rather a call to return to the chapters, rediscover the magic of classic songs, and honor the actual maestro who created the music and whose influence will continue to impact popular music for years to come.

Printed in Great Britain
by Amazon

43304168R00056